ONE, two, three, four,
Mary at the cottage door;
Five, six, seven, eight,
Eating cherries off a plate.

Dean's New Gift Book of Nursery Rhymes

Illustrated by

Janet & Anne Grahame Johnstone

PRINTED IN GREAT BRITAIN
DEAN & SON Ltd.
41/43 Ludgate Hill LONDON EC4
TRADE MARK

07503 7

O ALL you little
blackey-tops,
Pray don't eat my
father's crops,
While I lie down to
take a nap.
Shu-a-O! Shu-a-O!

LITTLE Jack Sprat
Once had a pig;
It was not very little,
Nor yet very big.
It was not very lean,
It was not very fat—
It's a good pig to grunt,
Said little Jack Sprat.

THE Man in the moon came tumbling down,
To ask his way to Norwich.
He went by the south and burnt his mouth,
By eating cold plum-porridge.

JENNY Wren fell sick
Upon a merry time,
In came Robin Redbreast
And brought her sops and wine.

Eat well of the sop, Jenny,
Drink well of the wine.
Thank you, Robin, kindly,
You shall be mine.

Jenny Wren got well,
And stood upon her feet;
And told Robin plainly,
She loved him not a bit.

Robin he got angry,
And hopped upon a twig,
Saying, Out upon you,
fie upon you!
Bold faced jig!

SING a song of sixpence,
A pocket full of rye;
Four-and-twenty blackbirds
Baked in a pie.

When the pie was opened
The birds began to sing;
Was not that a dainty dish
To set before the king?

The king was in his counting-house,
Counting out his money;

The queen was in the parlour,
  Eating bread and honey.

The maid was in the garden
Hanging out the clothes;
Down came a blackbird,
And pecked off her nose.

THE man in the wilderness asked of me,
How many strawberries grew in the sea.
I answered him,
As I thought good,
As many as red herrings
Grew in the wood.

PAT-A-CAKE, pat-a-cake, baker's man!
Make me a cake as fast as you can.
Pat it, and prick it, and mark it with T,
And put it in the oven for Tommy and me.

JACK SPRATT could eat no fat,
His wife could eat no lean,
And so, between them both,
They licked the platter clean.

THERE was an old woman who lived under a hill,
And if she's not gone, she's living there still.

GO to bed first,
A Golden Purse;

Go to bed second,
A Golden Pheasant;
Go to bed third,
A Golden Bird.

HERE am I, little Jumping Joan,
When I'm by myself, I'm all alone.

PLEASE to remember
The Fifth of November,
Gunpowder treason and plot;
I see no reason
Why Gunpowder Treason
Should ever be forgot.

DAME TROT and her cat
Sat down to chat;
The Dame sat on this side
And puss sat on that.

"Puss," says the Dame,
"Can you catch a rat
Or a mouse in the dark?"
"Purr!" says the cat.

LITTLE Tommy Tucker
Sings for his supper,
What shall we give him?
White bread and butter.
How shall he cut it
Without e're a knife?
How shall he marry
Without e're a wife?

"WHO goes there?"
"A Grenadier."
"What do you want?"
"A pot of beer."

MOLLY, my sister, and I fell out,
And what do you think it was all about?
She loved coffee and I loved tea,
And that was the reason we could not agree.

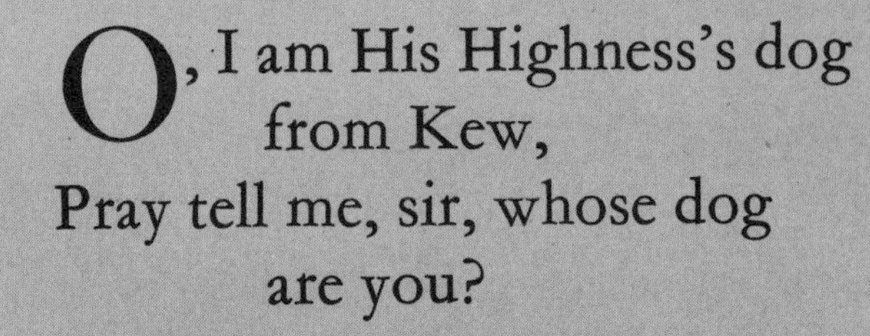

O, I am His Highness's dog
from Kew,
Pray tell me, sir, whose dog
are you?

THE Robin and the Wren
Fought about the porridge-pan;
And ere the Robin got a spoon
The Wren had ate the porridge down.

HERE'S sulky Sue!
What shall we do?
Put her in the corner, till
she comes to.

I'LL sing you a song,
Though not very long,
Yet I think it as pretty as any.
Put your hand in your purse,
You'll never be worse,
And give the poor singer a penny.

MILLIONS of massive raindrops
Have fallen all around;
They have danced on the house tops,
They have hidden in the ground.

They were liquid-like musicians,
With anything for keys,
Beating tunes upon the windows,
Keeping time upon the trees.

A NICK and a nock,
A hen and a cock,
And a penny for my master.

PETER, Peter, pumpkin eater,
Had a wife and couldn't keep her.
He put her in a pumpkin shell,
And there he kept her very well.

TWO little dicky birds
Sat upon a wall,

One called Peter
One called Paul.

Fly away Peter,
Fly away Paul;

Come back Peter,
Come back Paul.

SEE-SAW, scaradown,
Which is the way to London town?
One foot up, and the other foot down,
That is the way
to London town.

COBBLER, cobbler, mend my shoe,
Get it done by half-past two;
Stitch it up, and stitch it down,
And then I'll give you half a crown.

LUCY LOCKET lost her
pocket,
Kitty Fisher found it:
Not a penny in her purse,
But a ribbon round it.

THERE was a little boy and a little girl
Lived in our alley;
Says the little boy to the little girl,
"Shall I, oh, shall I?"
Says the little girl to the little boy,
"What shall we do?"
Says the little boy to the little girl,
"I will kiss you!"

HOT cross buns,
Hot cross buns,
One a penny, two a penny,
Hot cross buns;
If your daughters don't like them,
Give them to your sons.
One a penny, two a penny,
Hot cross buns.

ROCK-A-BYE baby, thy
cradle is green,
Father's a nobleman,
mother's a Queen.
Johnny's a drummer, and
drums for the King
And Betty's a lady, and
wears a gold ring.

PUNCH and Judy
Fought for a pie;
Punch gave Judy
A knock in the eye.

A WISE owl lived in an oak;
The more he saw the less he
spoke;
The less he spoke the more he heard.
Why can't we all be like that wise
old bird?

I'LL tell you a story of Jack-a-Nory,
And now my story's begun.
I'll tell you another of Jack and his
brother,
And now my story's done.

WARM hands, warm the men are gone
to plough.
If you want to warm your hands, warm your
hands now.

GIRLS and boys come out to play,
The moon doth shine as bright as day.
Come with a whoop and come with a call;
Come with a good will or not at all.

Up the ladder and down the wall,
A halfpenny roll will serve us all;
You find milk and I'll find flour,
And we'll have a pudding in half an hour.

FINEST
FLOUR

"PRETTY maid, pretty maid,
Where have you been?"
"Gathering a posie
To give to the Queen."

"Pretty maid, pretty maid,
What gave she you?"
"She gave me a diamond
As big as my shoe."

PEASE pudding hot, pease pudding cold,
Pease pudding in the pot, nine days old.
Some like it hot, some like it cold,
Some like it in the pot, nine days old.

BABY shall have an apple,
Baby shall have a plum,
Baby shall have a rattle,
When Daddy comes home.

A MAN of words and not
of deeds
Is like a garden full
of weeds!

YOUNG lambs to sell,
young lambs to sell,
If I'd as much money as I
could tell;
I wouldn't be crying, "Young
lambs to sell."

A PIE sat on a pear tree.
A pie sat on a pear tree.
Heigh O, heigh O, heigh O.
Once so merrily hopped she.
Twice so merrily hopped she,
Thrice so merrily hopped she,
Heigh O, heigh O, heigh O.

JINGLE bells, Jingle bells
Jingle all the way.
O what fun it is to ride
In a one-horse open sleigh.

THERE was an old woman and what do
you think?
She lived on nothing but victuals and drink.
Victuals and drink were the chief of her diet,
Yet this plaguy old woman could never be quiet.

NOW we dance looby looby,
Now we dance looby light;
Now we dance looby, looby looby,
Now we dance looby yester-night.

Shake your right hand a little,
Shake your left hand a little,
Shake your head a little,
And turn you round about.

WYNKEN, Blynken, and Nod one night
Sailed off in a wooden shoe—
Sailed on a river of crystal light,
Into a sea of dew.
"Where are you going, and what do you wish?"
The old moon asked the three.
"We have come to fish for the herring fish
That live in this beautiful sea;
Nets of silver and gold have we!"
Said Wynken,
Blynken,
And Nod.

The old moon laughed and sang a song,
As they rocked in the wooden shoe,
And the wind that sped them all night long
Ruffled the waves of dew.
The little stars were the herring fish
That lived in that beautiful sea—
"Now cast your nets wherever you wish—
Never afeard are we;"
So cried the stars to the fishermen three:
Wynken,
Blynken,
And Nod.

All night long their nets they threw
To the stars in the twinkling foam—
Then down from the skies came the wooden shoe,
Bringing the fishermen home;
'Twas all so pretty a sail it seemed
As if it could not be,
And some folks thought 'twas a dream they
        dreamed
Of sailing that beautiful sea—
But I shall name you the fishermen three:
        Wynken,
        Blynken,
        And Nod.

Wynken and Blynken are two little eyes,
And Nod is a little head,
And the wooden shoe that sailed the skies
Is a wee one's trundle bed.
So shut your eyes while Mother sings
Of wonderful sights that be,
And you shall see the beautiful things
As you rock in the misty sea,
Where the old shoe rocked the fishermen three:

Wynken,
Blynken,
And Nod.

DRIBBLE, dribble, trickle, trickle,
What a lot of sawdust.
My dolly's had an accident,
And lost a lot of sawdust.

I OFTEN sit and wish that I
Could be a kite up in the sky,
And ride upon the breeze, and go
Whatever way it chanced to blow;
Then I could look beyond the town,
And see the river winding down,
And follow all the ships that sail,
Like me, before the merry gale,
Until like them at last I came
To some place with a foreign name.

A FROG he would a-wooing go,
Heigho, says Rowley;
Whether his mother would let him or no:
With a roly, poly, gammon, and spinach,
Heigho, says Anthony Rowley.

So off he went with his opera hat,
Heigho, says Rowley;
And on the road he met with a rat,
With a roly, poly, gammon, and spinach,
Heigho, says Anthony Rowley.

"Pray, Mr. Rat, will you go with me,"
Heigho, says Rowley;
"Kind Mrs. Mousey for to see?"
With a roly, poly, gammon, and spinach,
Heigho, says Anthony Rowley.

When they came to the door at Mousey's hall,
Heigho, says Rowley;
They gave a loud tap, and they gave a loud call,
With a roly, poly, gammon, and spinach,
Heigho, says Anthony Rowley.

"Pray, Mrs. Mouse, are you within?"
Heigho, says Rowley;
"Yes, kind sirs, and sitting to spin,"
With a roly, poly, gammon, and spinach,
Heigho says, Anthony Rowley.

"Pray, Mrs. Mouse, now give us some beer,"
Heigho, says Rowley;
"For Froggy and I are fond of good cheer,"
With a roly, poly, gammon, and spinach,
Heigho, says Anthony Rowley.

"Pray Mr. Frog, will you give us a song?"
Heigho, says Rowley;
"But let it be something that's not very long,"
With a roly, poly, gammon, and spinach,
Heigho, says Anthony Rowley.

"Indeed, Miss Mouse," replied Mr. Frog,
Heigho, says Rowley;
"A cold has made me as hoarse as a hog,"
With a roly, poly, gammon, and spinach,
Heigho, says Anthony Rowley.

"Since you've caught cold, Mr. Frog," Mousey said,
Heigho, says Rowley;
"I'll sing you a song that I have just made,"
With a roly, poly, gammon, and spinach,
Heigho, says Anthony Rowley.

But while they were all a-merrymaking,
Heigho, says Rowley;
A Cat and her Kittens came tumbling in,
With a roly, poly, gammon, and spinach,
Heigho, says Anthony Rowley.

The Cat she seized the Rat by the crown,
Heigho says, Rowley;
The Kittens they pulled the little Mouse down,
With a roly, poly, gammon, and spinach,
Heigho, says Anthony Rowley.

This put Mr. Frog in a terrible fright,
    Heigho, says Rowley;
He took up his hat and he wished them good night,
    With a roly, poly, gammon, and spinach,
Heigho, says Anthony Rowley.

As Froggy was crossing a silvery brook,
    Heigho, says Rowley;
A lily-white Duck came and gobbled him up,
    With a roly, poly, gammon, and spinach,
Heigho, says Anthony Rowley.

So here is an end of one, two, and three—
    Heigho, says Rowley;
The Rat, the Mouse, and the little Froggy,
    With a roly, poly, gammon, and spinach,
Heigho, says Anthony Rowley.

THE gossips of the village—see,
Their fine lace caps are wearing.
They sip their dainty cups of tea,
White sugar they are sharing.

Their fingers shine with golden rings,
But—duty never matters!
Nothing is ready for the men
And under—they are tatters.

CHARLEY PARLEY stole the barley
Out of the baker's shop.
The baker came out, and gave him a clout,
Which made poor Charley hop.

THIS is the
House that
Jack built.

This is the Malt
That lay in the house that Jack built.

This is the Rat, that ate the malt,
That lay in the house that Jack built.

This is the Cat that killed
the rat,
That ate the malt,
That lay in the house
that Jack built.

This is the Dog that worried
the cat,
That killed the rat, that
ate the malt,
That lay in the house that Jack built.

This is the Cow with the crumpled horn,
That tossed the dog, that worried the cat,
That killed the rat, that ate the malt,
That lay in the house that Jack built.

This is the Maiden all forlorn,
That milked the cow with the crumpled horn,
That tossed the dog, that worried the cat,
That killed the rat, that ate the malt,
That lay in the house that Jack built.

This is the Man all tattered and torn,
That kissed the maiden all forlorn,
That milked the cow with the crumpled horn,
That tossed the dog, that worried the cat,
That killed the rat, that ate the malt,
That lay in the house that Jack built.

This is the Priest all shaven and shorn,
That married the man all tattered and torn,
That kissed the maiden all forlorn,
That milked the cow with the crumpled horn,
That tossed the dog, that worried the cat,
That killed the rat, that ate the malt,
That lay in the house that Jack built.

This is the Cock that crowed in the morn,
That waked the priest all shaven and shorn,
That married the man all tattered and torn,
That kissed the maiden all forlorn,
That milked the cow with the crumpled horn,
That tossed the dog, that worried the cat,
That killed the rat, that ate the malt,
That lay in the house that Jack built.

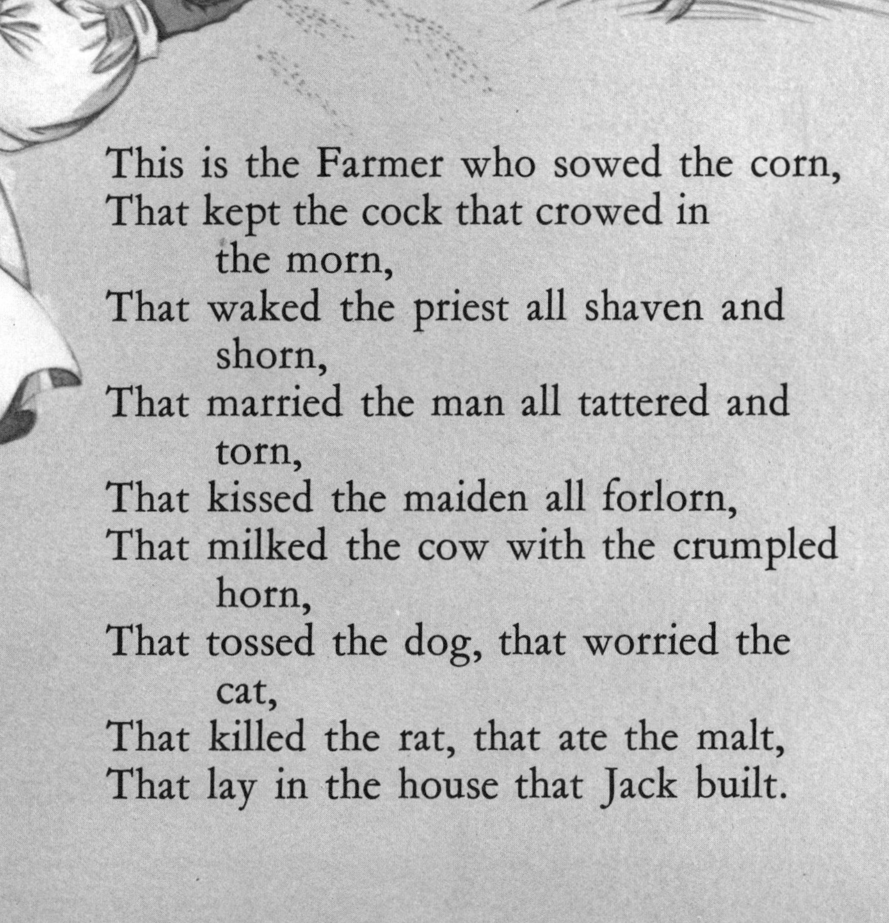

This is the Farmer who sowed the corn,
That kept the cock that crowed in
the morn,
That waked the priest all shaven and
shorn,
That married the man all tattered and
torn,
That kissed the maiden all forlorn,
That milked the cow with the crumpled
horn,
That tossed the dog, that worried the
cat,
That killed the rat, that ate the malt,
That lay in the house that Jack built.

A PILLOW shaken in the sky,
See how all the feathers fly,
Little snowflakes soft and light
Make the trees and meadows white.

SWING high, swing low, away we go,
Up to the trees where the breezes blow,
Where the birdies nest and play all day,
And all the world is bright and gay.

Swing high, swing low, away we go,
High up where the leaves do grow.
All the little birds are singing,
As we gaily go a-swinging.